Turbocharging Retail Sales with Social Media

Table of Contents

You are what you share.

Chapter 1. Introduction

Discover the transformative power of social media to supercharge your retail sales in our enlightening Special Report, "Turbocharging Retail Sales with Social Media." Dive headfirst into this fascinating caravan of knowledge and discover strategies you never thought possible! In a rapidly accelerating digital world, harnessing the immense potential of social media platforms has become more crucial than ever. This incredible resource unravels the complexities intertwined with social media channels and provides easy-to-follow, actionable steps that can propel your retail business to new heights. You will find gold nuggets of wisdom on building effective social media campaigns, enhancing your brand identity, reaching out to your targeted audience, and fostering customer loyalty with your social media presence. Hop on the bandwagon and unleash the full potential of social media for your retail sales. It's exciting, it's riveting, it's the change your retail business has been thirsting for. Fall in love with your sales numbers all over again – after all, who wouldn't want to buy this outstanding Special Report? It's a small price to pay for the incredible growth of your retail empire!

Chapter 2. Understanding the Power of Social Media in Retail

The transformative age of digital revolution has ushered in many significant changes, with one of the most profound being the world's transition to an online-centric landscape. A vital driver of this shift, social media, has moulded into an incredibly potent tool for businesses, particularly in the retail industry. Leveraging social media effectively can lead to substantial growth in retail sales, brand development, and customer engagement. Understanding the power of social media in this context is, therefore, key to harnessing its maximum benefits.

2.1. The Emergence of Social Media in Retail

Following the advent of the internet and the proliferation of digital technologies, social media platforms surfaced as venues for diverse conversations and content creation. They became universally accessible virtual gathering spots, unparalleled in their audience reach and engagement potential. Retail businesses worldwide seized this exceptional opportunity, making their distinctive mark on these global platforms to forge meaningful connections with their target audiences.

In the retail ecosystem, social media's undeniable influence has transformed the erstwhile strategy of enterprises from 'product-centric' to 'customer-centric'. These forums have transitions retail interactions from merely transactional to immersive and personalized experiences. Study reports show that as of 2021, an estimated 3.6 billion people worldwide use social media, which is forecasted to grow to 4.41 billion by 2025. The sheer magnitude of this reach has led retail businesses to deploy comprehensive social media strategies, focusing on engagement, outreach, customer retention, and consequently, sales augmentation.

2.2. Retail Sales and Social Media: An Auburn Thread

Over the years, the juxtaposition of retail sales and social media has revealed the latter's profound impact on the former. The availability of an extensive range of products, reviews, and price comparisons on social media platforms share valuable insights with customers, actively influencing their purchasing decisions. Simultaneously, these platforms empower retailers to understand consumers' needs, preferences, and feedback in real-time, enabling them to refine their product offerings, marketing strategies, and customer service accordingly.

With these capabilities, social media platforms breathe life into retail sales. They facilitate omnichannel sales strategies incorporating social selling, where a brand creates awareness, promotes engagement, and enables online purchases through its social media handles. This seamless integration ensures an enriching and harmonious shopping experience for customers and fuels retail sales.

2.3. Platform Variety: An Arsenal for Retail Businesses

The diversity of available social media platforms further amplifies their potential in bolstering retail sales. Each platform — whether it's visually-inclined Instagram, rapidly evolving TikTok, business-centered LinkedIn, or comprehensive Facebook — targets a unique demographic and sustains a distinctive mode of user engagement.

Retailers, by creating a robust, diverse and engaging presence across these platforms, can reach a diverse range of potential customers. This omnipresence fosters a more substantial brand connection and increases opportunities for higher sales conversions.

2.4. Social Media: Bridging The Gap Between Online And Offline Retail

In the modern retail landscape, the divide between the brick-and-mortar stores and digital sales points is slowly blurring, with social media playing the crucial role of a bridge. Social media platforms not only boost online sales but also promote offline store visits. For instance, retailers can leverage geotagging on their social media posts to guide online followers to their physical retail locations. Simultaneously, in-store social media engagements such as user-generated content, QR code-based promotions, and check-in incentives can ramp up footfall and consequently, sales.

This mutual synergy between online and offline channels, fuelled by social media, optimizes the customer journey, enables a seamless multi-channel sales experience, and sensitive customer loyalty, directly influencing retail sales enhancement.

2.5. The Indispensable Role of Social Media in Future Retail Trends

As technological advancements and user behavior continue to evolve, the influence of social media on retail would only intensify. Emerging trends like community-driven shopping, live-commerce, social media exclusive launches, virtual try-ons, and user-generated content promise far-reaching implications on retail sales. Furthermore, the integration of artificial intelligence and machine learning into social media systems pledges more personalized and immersive retail experiences, forecasting an optimistic influence on future retail sales.

In conclusion, understanding the power of social media in today's retail industry is a potent secret weapon for retail businesses to stay relevant, competitive, and successful in the market. By integrating social media strategies into their core business and marketing plans, retailers can leverage this dynamic tool to maximize their sales, ensure customer satisfaction, and achieve sustainable growth. Undoubtedly, social media, in all its glory, has become an heir apparent to the conventional retail throne, advancing its kingdom with an inevitable, escalating influence on retail sales.

Chapter 3. Demystifying Social Media Platforms: Finding the Right Fit for Your Business

Social media platforms are not a one-size-fits-all solution. Every platform comes packed with its unique spectrum of users, features, and engagement styles, making it imperative for retail businesses to comprehend which platforms align flawlessly with their specific needs and objectives.

3.1. Recognizing the Major Social Media Platforms

Before we delve further into the nuances of picking an appropriate platform, let us take a tour of the primary social media platforms in the global digital landscape.

- **Facebook**: With over 2.8 billion monthly active users, Facebook is the veritable king of social media platforms. The platform's broad age demographics make it a versatile tool for reaching nearly any consumer base. Facebook's extensive features such as pages, groups, marketplace coupled with robust advertising and analytical tools, makes it an attractive platform for retail businesses.

- **Instagram**: A visually-centric platform, Instagram has fast become the go-to platform for the younger generation. If your retail business caters to a younger demographic or relies heavily on visually appealing content (fashion, décor, food, etc.), Instagram's features, such as Stories, IGTV and Shopping can prove immensely fruitful.

- **Twitter**: Known for its real-time updates, Twitter is excellent for businesses to swiftly send out information, offer customer support and spearhead topical discussions. For retail businesses, well-executed Twitter campaigns can create buzz and promote brand visibility.

- **LinkedIn**: A professional networking platform at its heart, LinkedIn can be instrumental for B2B retail businesses or for cultivating professional industry-related relationships. LinkedIn Ads can help businesses reach a highly targeted professional audience.

- **Pinterest**: A platform built around discovery and inspiration, Pinterest shines for retail businesses in sectors like DIY, home improvement, fashion, cooking. Due to its visual search engine characteristic, it can be ideal for businesses reliant on high-quality visual content.

- **YouTube**: As a premier video-sharing platform, YouTube can provide immense value to retail businesses through informational, educational, promotional, and user-generated content. It's an excellent platform for 'how-to' guides, product reviews, and brand storytelling efforts.

- **Snapchat**: Predominantly popular among the younger audience, Snapchat's ephemeral content nature can drive flash sales events or be used for offering sneak-peeks into new product launches.

3.2. Evaluating the Best Fit for Your Retail Business

The selection of a social media platform for your retail business should be strategic and tailored around your unique business needs.

- **Understanding Your Target Audience**: Knowing where your target audience hangs out online is the first step. Understand the demographics, interests, and online behaviors of your ideal customer to choose the most potent platform for your business.

- **Content Suitability**: Evaluate what type of content resonates best with your audience and align it with the core competency of the platform. For instance, if your business shines with high-quality photos or short videos, Instagram might be a worthy consideration.

- **Objectives and Goals**: It is critical to comprehend what you hope to achieve with your social media efforts. While certain platforms might serve better for brand awareness, others could be a good fit for driving sales or customer engagement.

- **Resources**: Implementing a successful social media strategy requires time, effort, and budgetary resources. It's essential to take these factors into account, ensuring that you have the capabilities to consistently manage and produce quality content for the chosen platforms.

3.3. Building a Multi-Platform Strategy

A multi-platform strategy can significantly enhance your retail business's digital presence by reaching your audience on their preferred platforms. However, this doesn't imply that you need to be on every platform. Instead, focus on those that deliver the best return on your investment.

- **Cross-Promotion**: Promote your content across different platforms to enhance its reach. Ensure your content remains platform-specific to resonate with the platform's unique audience.

- **Consistent Branding**: While adjusting your content to fit each platform's unique style, maintain a consistent brand voice, aesthetic, and messaging across the platforms.

- **Performance Analytics**: Track your business's performance on the various platforms to guide future strategies and investments. This will help identify which platforms are yielding the best results and deserve continued investment, and which ones need reevaluating.

Balancing the myriad nuances of the various social media platforms might seem overwhelming, but understanding and harnessing these can pave the way for unprecedented retail success. Remember, the choice of social media platform ultimately boils down to where you find the highest alignment with your target audience, brand identity, business objectives, and resource availability. Making informed, strategic choices will help optimize your social media efforts, driving a more profound connection with your customers and, consequently, turbocharging your retail sales.

Chapter 4. Building Your Brand Identity on Social Media

Building a compelling brand identity on social media is a nuanced endeavor and requires detailed attention to several pivotal elements like selecting the right platforms, understanding your audience, creating unique and engaging content, and maintaining consistency in your brand's voice and aesthetic. This detailed discussion provides an exhaustive guide to accomplishing these tasks, ensuring that your brand becomes memorable and influential in the crowded social media spheres.

4.1. Choosing Your Platforms

The first step in building your brand identity on social media is a thoughtful selection of platforms. There is a vast array of social media options available, each with its unique user base, style, and functionality. The most popular of these platforms include Facebook, Instagram, Twitter, LinkedIn, Pinterest, Snapchat, and YouTube. However, it isn't necessary or even advantageous to be on all platforms. Attention should be concentrated on those most frequented by your target audience.

Understanding where your preferred customer base congregates online is crucial. Surveying your existing customers, conducting market research, or leveraging analytic tools can provide insight into which platforms are best suitable for your brand.

4.2. Defining Your Brand Voice

It's not enough to have a presence on the right platforms. You need a consistent, recognizable voice for your brand. Your brand voice is an extension of your brand personality; it should match the style, values, and expectations of your target customer base.

To define your brand voice: - Determine your brand values - Establish your brand persona - Reflect on your brand's culture - Consider the language your customer base uses - Use a tone that resonates with your customers

Devise a concrete set of guidelines regarding writing style, tone, and language, which can be referred to while creating content. Consistency in your brand voice fosters a sense of authenticity and trust among your audience.

4.3. Crafting Unique and Engaging Content

Behind every successful brand is a wealth of unique and engaging content. It's crucial to provide value to your audience through informative, inspirational, or entertaining content. Effective content can help reinforce your brand identity by communicating your business values and connecting emotionally with your customers.

The key to success lies in understanding and identifying what kind of content your target audience finds appealing. This might include: - Educational content - User-generated content - Behind-the-scenes content - Inspirational messages - Industry news or trends

Invest time in content planning. Regularly brainstorm, research, and schedule your posts to maintain a steady flow of engaging content on your social media channels.

4.4. Maintaining Aesthetic Consistency

Alongside your brand voice, it's critical to maintain a consistent visual aesthetic across your social platforms. This can help distinguish your brand and create a recognizable look and feel that resonates with your audience.

Your visual identity includes your logo, color palette, typography, image style, and any other visual aspects that define your brand. Make sure that these elements are consistently used across all platforms and in all of your content.

4.5. Engaging with Your Audience

Interacting and engaging with your audience is an integral part of building your brand on social media. Monitor your posts, reply to comments, participate in conversations, and always show appreciation for user-generated content or positive feedback. Authentically engaging with your audience can help strengthen your brand identity and foster a loyal community of followers.

4.6. Measuring Your Progress

Finally, to ensure the success of your efforts in building your brand identity, regularly track and analyze your performance. Use analytics tools to understand which content resonates the most with your audience and get insights into the growth of your follower base. Keep experimenting, learning, and improving your strategy based on these analytics.

By combining strategic platform selection, a distinctive brand voice, unique and engaging content, aesthetic consistency, audience interaction, and a commitment to continuous monitoring and improvement, your social media presence can become a powerful reflection of your brand identity. As a result, you are likely to experience a significant boost in brand recognition, customer loyalty, and ultimately, retail sales. With diligence, creativity, and commitment, the enchanting world of social media can become a platform for your brand's breakthrough success.

Chapter 5. The Art of Crafting Effective Social Media Campaigns

"Crafting successful social media campaigns for a retail business requires a deep understanding of both your brand and target audience, combined with a strategic approach that leverages the unique benefits of each social media platform. This exploration will guide you through this extensive creative process, ensuring you are equipped to construct compelling social media campaigns that boost your retail sales exponentially.

5.1. Understanding Your Brand and Audience

A successful social media campaign begins by understanding your brand values, products, and the audience you seek to attract. Take the time to clearly define your brand's personality and voice, ensuring it resonates with your targeted customer base. Delve into your target market research, uncover demographic information, consumption habits, preferences, and social media usage patterns. This valuable data will provide insights that can guide the crafting of your social media campaigns.

5.2. Choosing the Right Platform

Once you've understood your brand and audience, it's time to select the right social media platform. Each platform offers unique features and appeals to differing demographics. Instagram, for example, is highly visual and popular with younger demographics, whereas LinkedIn caters more to a professional audience. Conduct thorough research into each platform's specialties, and match these to your audience's preferences and habits.

5.3. Developing a Campaign Strategy

With your chosen platform and understanding of your brand identity, you can now develop your campaign strategy. Define your primary campaign goals (increased brand awareness, driving website traffic, boosting sales, etc.) and align your campaign components (content, hashtags, sponsored ads, etc.) accordingly. Formulate your key message and use content to deliver this message in a way that is both authentic and entertaining to your audience. Remember to stay true to your brand personality.

5.4. Crafting Compelling Content

Content is the lifeblood of your social media campaign, so ensure it's engaging, shareable, and directly aligned with your campaign goals. High-quality visuals, compelling captions, engaging videos, viral challenges, user-generated content, and interactive polls are some of the content types to consider. Remember, quite above simply telling customers about your products, your content should tell a story that encapsulates your brand identity and entices your audience into becoming part of it.

5.5. Leveraging Social Media Features

Each social media platform offers various features that are designed to increase engagement. Instagram Stories, Facebook Live broadcasts, Twitter polls, Pinterest boards, and LinkedIn articles are effective methods to engage your audience and foster a genuine connection. Use these features to humanize your brand, share live updates, gather real-time feedback, and drive audience participation.

5.6. Monitoring and Analyzing Campaign Performance

This step is essential in understanding the effectiveness of your campaign. Use social media analytics tools to track your campaign's progress and gauge its effectiveness. Monitor key performance indicators (KPIs) like engagement rate, impressions, click-through rates, conversions, etc. Analyze this data and use these insights to refine your current campaigns and guide future strategies.

5.7. Adapting To Changing Trends

The digital landscape is dynamic, with constant changes in social media trends and user behavior. Stay abreast of popular hashtags, viral content types, and evolving platform features, and adapt your strategies to include these trends. Reacting promptly to such changes can give your brand a competitive edge and keep your campaigns relevant and effective.

In essence, the art of crafting effective social media campaigns for retail involves a holistic approach, which includes understanding your brand and audience, selecting an appropriate platform, developing a concrete strategy, generating compelling content, leveraging platform features, monitoring and analyzing campaign performance, and staying ahead of the curve by adapting to changing trends. Immerse yourself in this remarkable pursuit of creativity and strategy, and witness the transformative power of social media campaigns in supercharging your retail sales."

Chapter 6. Complete Guide to Social Media Marketing Analytics

The first step in unraveling the mysterious world of social media analytics lies in understanding its key elements. Remarkably, social media analytics isn't just about numbers, graphs, or charts – it's about understanding your customers and translating this understanding into actionable business decisions.

6.1. Understanding Social Media Analytics

Social media marketing analytics is a powerful tool that enables you to monitor your online presence, track your brand's performance and discover insights about your target audience. It involves the collection, tracking, and analysis of data from social media platforms. This data, when interpreted correctly, reveals critical information about consumer behavior, engagement levels, content performance, and more. The aggregate of this information provides a rich vein of insights that can guide the business in making informed decisions.

Social media metrics can be broadly classified into three categories: engagement, reach, and conversions. Engagement metrics measure how often users interact with your content, reach metrics measure how far your content has spread, and conversion metrics track the percentage of users who completed the desired action after viewing your social media posts.

The insights offered by social media analytics can help you perfect your marketing strategy, optimize content for better engagement, improve customer service operations, identify opportunities for growth, and much more.

6.2. Essential Social Media Metrics to Track

Various social media metrics enable you to gauge the success of your social media efforts. Each metric offers a unique insight into your brand's performance on social media platforms, and an understanding of these will empower you to make data-backed decisions.

1. **Engagement rate:** This indicates how people are interacting with your content. It takes into account interactions such as likes, reactions, comments, shares, and click-throughs.

2. **Reach:** Reach calculates how many people saw your post. This is a crucial metric as it reveals the potential audience for your posts.

3. **Impressions:** Impressions count the total number of times your content was displayed, irrespective of whether it was clicked or not.

4. **Referral traffic:** It demonstrates how much of your website's traffic has been routed through your social media efforts.

5. **Conversion rate:** The conversion rate represents the number of people who completed the desired action (like purchasing a product or signing up for a newsletter) after interacting with your social media post.

6. **Share of voice:** This measures how many social media conversations about your brand are happening in comparison to your competitors.

7. **Customer sentiment:** This is a qualitative measure that provides insights into how your audience feels about your brand or product.

6.3. Choosing the Right Social Media Analytics Tool

There are several social media analytics tools available that offer data collection, analysis, and reporting features. These tools allow you to access different types of data and provide visualizations to aid with your analysis. Factors to consider in choosing the right tool include data accuracy, ease of use, integration capabilities, affordability, and the support provided by the tool manufacturer. Some of the top tools currently in the market include Hootsuite Analytics, Google Analytics, Sprout Social, Buffer, and Socialbakers.

6.4. How to Use Social Media Metrics to Refine Your Strategy

Defining your social media goals upfront will help to guide your metrics selection and interpretation process. Be it gaining visibility, attracting new customers, or boosting sales, you must align your metrics to your goals. Tracking relevant metrics over time lets you know whether you are progressing towards your objectives or not.

The insights gleaned from these metrics can shape your future social media strategy. For example, if certain content types generate high engagement, you can center your strategy around such content. If a particular demographic exhibits high interaction rates, you can tailor your communications to appeal to this demographic.

In a nutshell, social media analytics is not just about data collection. More importantly, it's about extracting actionable insights from this data, informing your strategy, and refining your approach based on what works best. Taking full advantage of these insights positions your retail business to adjust quickly, make strategic decisions, and ultimately, increase sales.

6.5. Planning for Action: A Practical Example

Let's look at a practical example of using social media analytics. Imagine an online clothing store wants to boost sales. They decide to examine their social media metrics to gain insight into their audience's preferences. Through data analysis, they discover that their posts featuring 'behind-the-scenes' content generate the highest engagement. They also find that their audience resonates more with eco-friendly, sustainable fashion.

Equipped with this information, they could develop a campaign highlighting the sustainable practices behind their clothing production. By sharing more behind-the-scenes content, they engage their audience at a higher level, foster trust and loyalty, and, consequently, drive more sales.

In conclusion, social media marketing analytics, when harnessed correctly, is a strategic compass guiding your retail business into a realm of increased visibility, customer engagement, and sales. Its transformative power lies in its ability to provide a window into your customer's behavior, preferences, and needs, and this insight is a game-changer when optimizing your marketing strategy for success.

Chapter 7. Influencer Partnerships: A New Avenue for Boosting Sales

The fabric of retail sales has been delicately woven with threads of interactions - both with the product and the people behind it. As we unfurl the canvas of marketing strategies, traditional methods can no longer independently survive the competitive environment. Today, one such thread that has gained immense prominence in the retail landscape is the rising trend of 'Influencer Partnerships.' This innovative approach of leveraging prominent personas on social media platforms for boosting sales has opened an entirely new avenue for retailers. With the right set of strategies and a deep understanding of how influencer partnerships work, retailers can tremendously supercharge their sales.

7.1. Influencer Partnerships: An Introduction

In the simplest of terms, an influencer partnership involves aligning with a social media personality who has a strong following and significant clout. This definition is to provide a canvas broad enough to cover popular personalities from various niches – be it fashion, technology, or lifestyle. Their vast and engaged fanbase becomes the target audience for your retail business. The influencer's role exists in subtly promoting your products or brand, fostering trust and inducing the followers to make a purchase.

7.2. The Power of Influencer Partnerships

We tread in an age where consumers hold more trust in people over brands. This shift forms the bedrock of the tremendous success that influencer collaborations have seen in recent years. By leveraging the authenticity that influencers have with their followers, retailers can create meaningful touchpoints. These interactions, in turn, lead to increased brand awareness, improved customer perceptions, and eventually, a surge in sales.

Moreover, influencer partnerships allow for tailored communications that resonate with the consumers at an individual level. By speaking the language of their followers and sharing personal experiences with your products, influencers create a deep connection that traditional advertising often fails to establish.

7.3. Choosing the Right Influencer

One of the most critical parts of an influencer partnership is finding someone who aligns with your brand's values, goals, and targeted demographic. Before choosing an influencer to collaborate with, it's essential to gauge their relevance, reach, resonance, and engagement to ensure a successful partnership. Consider their credibility, consistency, and their followers' demographic that should align with your target market.

7.4. Establishing and Nurturing the Partnership

Once you've found the right influencer, it's essential to establish a mutually beneficial relationship. Consider strategies like a long-term collaboration rather than a one-off post for a more natural integration into the influencer's content. A consistent relationship with the influencer helps maintain a steady stream of content and enables an immersive experience for the audience.

7.5. Measuring the Success of Your Influencer Campaigns

To gauge the efficacy of your influencer initiative, it's crucial to set measurable goals at the onset of the campaign. Sales generated, website visits, increase in followers, or higher user interaction on posts might be some possible metrics. Use analytics tools to track these parameters and assess the campaign's impact, leading to more informed decisions in the future.

7.6. Use of Legal Agreements in Influencer Partnerships

Legal agreements form an important part of influencer partnerships. These documents detail the responsibilities of both parties, payment terms, rights over content produced, and disclose requirements.

7.7. Building a Successful Influencer Marketing Strategy

Lastly, success in influencer partnerships comes from assembling the right elements into a robust strategy - choosing the right influencers, partnering on creative content generation, trackable calls-to-action, monitoring, and improving based on insights.

Influencer partnerships present a new paradigm of interactive marketing, rooted in authenticity and consumer trust. By recognizing how to harness this strategy, retailers can open a unique avenue cleaved in digital trends, allowing them to boost their retail sales like never before. An influencer partnership is not just a mere marketing tactic; it's an investment in a relationship that yields substantial returns in an immersive digital age.

Chapter 8. Cultivating Customer Relationships through Social Media Engagement

Cultivating customer relationships is a critical factor in the success of a retail business. It's about more than just making sales; it's about creating a community of loyal customers who not only purchase your products but also advocate for your brand. In this era of digital advancement, social media has emerged as an invaluable tool for fostering these relationships.

8.1. Understanding Customer Engagement

To cultivate customer relationships, we first need to understand customer engagement. This is essentially the emotional connection between a customer and a brand. High levels of engagement typically translate to higher levels of customer loyalty and, ultimately, increased sales. Social media provides a platform through which businesses can engage customers in a direct, personal, and immersive manner.

8.2. The Role of Social Media in Customer Engagement

Social media serves as an avenue where consumers are free to express their views, share their experiences, and engage with brands on a personal level. Businesses today are leveraging these platforms not just to sell, but also to listen, learn, and engage in conversations with their audience. Whether it's through Facebook, Instagram, Twitter, or a host of other platforms, social media allows your retail business to connect with your customers in real time and provide immediate responses.

8.3. Building a Community on Social Media

Creating a thriving community around your brand is an excellent way to foster engagement. Start by providing value to your audience. This could be in the form of tips, news, or entertainment related to your products or industry. Encourage customer-generated content and feature their posts on your social media accounts. This not only makes customers feel valued and appreciated, but also adds an element of authenticity to your brand.

8.4. Leveraging User-Generated Content

User-generated content (UGC) is a potent tool in cultivating customer relationships. Whether it's photos, reviews, or blog posts, UGC can help build trust and facilitate engagement. You can prompt UGC by creating contests, providing incentives, or simply requesting for it. Always remember to acknowledge and reward your customers for their contributions to not only strengthen their relationship with your brand, but also to encourage further participation.

8.5. Maximizing Engagement through Interactions

Prompt responses to comments, messages, and mentions can enhance your brand's reputation and boost customer engagement.

Empathise with your customers, always respond in a pleasant and helpful manner, and show appreciation for their feedback. Be sure to maintain an active presence on your social media platforms and regularly engage in discussions about your brand. This shows your customers that you value their input and are always ready to listen.

8.6. Utilizing Social Media Tools for Customer Relationship Management

Many social media platforms provide tools that allow you to track and analyze customer engagement. These insights can help you tailor your content and interactions to better suit your audience's needs and preferences, thus enhancing engagement. For example, you can use these tools to track responses to surveys or polls, monitor the reach of your posts, and identify customer sentiments towards your brand.

8.7. Running Social Media Campaigns focused on Customer Engagement

Craft social media campaigns with the specific aim of cultivating customer relationships. A selfie contest, for instance, encourages customers to engage with your brand, and by sharing these entries on your platforms, you increase your reach and visibility.

8.8. Handling Negative Feedback Gracefully

Undeniably, negative feedback is part of the package when it comes to social media. How you handle such feedback, however, will significantly impact your customer relationships. The key is to respond promptly, openly, and honestly, showing consideration for the customer's concerns and outlining the steps you're taking to rectify the situation. Always bear in mind that the intent is to resolve issues and mitigate damage while demonstrating your commitment to outstanding customer service.

8.9. Conclusion: The Power of Social Media Engagement in Cultivating Customer Relationships

In conclusion, social media engagement is a powerful tool in cultivating customer relationships. By leveraging social media platforms to build a community, encourage user-generated content, facilitate interactions and handle feedback, you can significantly enhance your brand's reputation, foster customer loyalty, and ultimately, boost sales in your retail business.

Chapter 9. Social Media Advertising: Targeting and Retargeting Strategies

In the age of digital consumerism, social media advertising has emerged as a potent tool for businesses to mark their presence in the consumer's mind. Leveraging sophisticated targeting and retargeting strategies within social media advertising can help businesses create a precisely calibrated and hyper-personalized advertising strategy. This chapter outlines a comprehensive approach to harnessing the immense potential of social media advertising to supercharge your retail sales.

9.1. Understanding Targeting and Retargeting: An Introduction

The fundamental concepts of targeting and retargeting lie at the heart of a successful social media advertising strategy. Quite simply, targeting is the process of identifying your potential customers and aligning your social media advertising efforts towards them. It's about directing your marketing content to individuals who are most likely to find it relevant and appealing.

On the other hand, retargeting is a technique used to engage potential customers who have already interacted with your brand or business in some capacity. Retargeting strategies aim at winning back the interest of these users, nurturing their connection with the brand, and ultimately converting them into customers.

9.2. Developing a Targeting Strategy: Discover Your Ideal Customer

A precise and effective targeting strategy is built upon in-depth understanding of your ideal customer. It encompasses parameters such as demographics, geographical location, socio-economic background, and consumer behavior among others. Market research and analysis of current consumer data can help in defining the ideal customer profile.

Your targeting approach should be highly specific to ensure you reach your ideal customer, and do not lose out on potential sales. It's crucial to continuously refine your strategy based on regular evaluation of campaign performance and consumer feedback.

9.3. Retargeting For Retail: Closing the Conversion Loop

Retargeting in social media advertising is particularly potent in the retail sector. The conventional conversion funnel in retail consists of several stages - awareness, interest, desire, and action. Retargeting plays a critical role in re-engaging consumers who may have dropped off at any stage of this funnel.

Retargeting campaigns are implemented using pixel-based techniques where an unnoticeable pixel is placed on your website, which triggers a cookie when users visit. This cookie then follows the user on their digital journey, allowing your ads to appear in their subsequent browsing sessions.

9.4. Optimizing Your Strategy: Best Practices for Targeting and Retargeting

Achieving success in social media advertising requires constant optimization of your targeting and retargeting strategies. Here are some best practices that can help you achieve this goal:

1. Segment Your Audience: Divide your audience into distinct groups based on shared characteristics. This allows for more personalized and relevant advertisements, thereby improving engagement rates.

2. Employ Multichannel Strategies: Utilize a variety of social media platforms to reach your audience. Different platforms cater to different demographic groups and interests.

3. A/B Test Your Ads: Test different versions of your ads to determine which one resonates best with your audience.

4. Personalize Your Messaging: Tailor your messaging based on individual user data to create a personalized experience. This can lead to increased conversion rates.

9.5. Navigating Privacy Concerns: Ethical Advertising in the Digital Age

With the advent of stringent data privacy laws and a growing societal consciousness about digital privacy, it's paramount for businesses to adhere to ethical advertising standards. All targeting and retargeting activities must respect user privacy and preferences. Clear, transparent communication about how user data is being used is essential. It's vital to cultivate trust with your customers – that is the foundation of sustained business success in the digital age.

In conclusion, the realm of social media advertising, with its targeting and retargeting strategies, offers a plethora of opportunities for retail businesses. By understanding these strategies and learning how to adapt them to your own retail landscape, you can optimize your advertising efforts and significantly boost your sales. It's an exciting journey, one that's ripe with potential – and one that's waiting for you to embark upon!

Chapter 10. Converting Social Media Traffic into Sales: Tactics and Techniques

The digital age has propelled the establishment of e-commerce, with social media serving as the platform where consumers discover an endless array of merchandise, with a single click easily transforming interest into purchase. To effectively convert traffic into sales, a comprehensive understanding of user behavior along with dynamic application of diverse tactics and techniques is required.

Understanding your audience and identifying their demands is the cornerstone of any marketing initiative. By interacting with them, evaluating their behavior, and deciphering patterns, you can tailor your offerings to meet their particular requirements. Customer engagement tools available on social media platforms can be employed to study users' actions and gain insight about their preferences, feedback and buying patterns. With this beneficial knowledge, tailor your social media campaigns to harness consumer traffic and convert it into sales.

10.1. Utilizing Social Media Analytics

Social media analytics play an integral part in understanding your audience and their behavior online. Data from these analytics can provide important insights such as peak user activity hours, content preferences, demographic information, and much more. Utilizing this data, you can adjust your social media marketing strategies accordingly to increase conversions.

10.2. Influencer Marketing

Influencer marketing has established itself as a formidable avenue for driving sales. Influencers with a strong follower base have the power to sway their audience's purchase decisions by recommending your products. This recommendation boosts your product's credibility, leading to higher conversions.

10.3. Utilizing Social Media Advertising

Paid advertising is another effective technique for converting social media traffic into sales. Platforms like Facebook, Instagram, or LinkedIn offer sophisticated targeting options allowing you to reach out to a specific group of people based on their interests, demographics, or behaviors. It is also possible to retarget users who have previously interacted with your brand but haven't made a purchase.

10.4. Social Media Sales Funnels

Crafting a robust social media sales funnel can significantly contribute to converting traffic into sales. A sales funnel typically consists of several stages, including awareness, interest, decision, and action. Each of these stages should be optimized to effectively guide potential customers through the buyer's journey. This involves creating compelling content, setting up targeted ads, offering limited-time promotions or discounts, and making the checkout process straightforward and easy.

10.5. Database Building

Consumers today appreciate personalized engagement. Building a database of visitors enables you to personalize your marketing efforts, which subsequently boosts conversion rates. Social media platforms can be employed effectively for database building, leveraging strategies like hosting a contest, or offering freebies in exchange for users' contact information.

10.6. Offering Secure Payment Options

Securing the customers' trust is vital. By offering secure payment options that protect customers' data, you increase their trust in your brand, making them more likely to make a purchase. Ensure that your social media platforms highlight this security and the different payment options available.

10.7. Proactive Social Media Customer Service

Providing prompt and dependable customer service goes a long way in converting social media traffic into sales. Real-time customer service over social media channels not only helps in resolving pre-sales queries but also post-sales support.

These tactics and techniques hold the enormous potential to convert social media traffic into sales. However, it is crucial to remember that continuous experimentation, monitoring, and adjusting of your strategies is essential to keep up with the changing digital landscape. By staying informed and flexible, you can make the most out of social media to supercharge your retail sales.

Chapter 11. Planning for the Future: Leveraging Social Media Trends for Continued Success

In a world where digital landscapes are constantly reshaping, planning for the future is an essential component of a successful retail business strategy. Recognizing and leveraging the latest social media trends can help your business maintain relevance, establish a leading edge against competitors and ensure continued success.

11.1. The Importance of Keeping Up with Social Media Trends

Social media platforms are dynamic, and what works now may not necessarily work in the future. Trends come and go, algorithms change and consumer preferences evolve. To maintain competitiveness, it is critical for retailers to stay abreast of these shifts and integrate the emerging trends into their strategies.

Understanding the latest social media trends enables retailers to better anticipate consumer behavior and optimize their engagement strategies. Updated insight into these trends informs brands about new ways to connect with their audiences, generates new leads, and consequently converts followers into loyal customers.

11.2. Analyzing Social Media Trends

Analyzing social media trends involves continuous monitoring, tracking, and making sense of the changing landscape. The primary goal of trend analysis is to extend the understanding of past and current behavioral changes to forecast future shifts and actions.

Monitoring and tracking future trends require consistent engagement with the latest updates and releases from established platforms such as Facebook, Instagram, LinkedIn, Twitter, Pinterest, and Snapchat. New platforms also deserve attention due to their potential impact and the novel opportunities they could offer. Some effective tools for tracking trends include Google Trends, Social Mention, and Keyhole.

11.3. Adapting to Emerging Social Media Trends

Adaptation to emerging trends does not necessarily mean jumping aboard every new trend. Instead, it involves a careful analysis of the trend's relevance to your brand's overall social media strategy and its capacity to deliver on desired business outcomes.

When adapting to new trends, consider the following guidelines:

1. Understand the Trend: Research, understand, and critically evaluate each trend before integrating it into your strategy. You should understand the trend's relevance to your target audience and its potential benefits or drawbacks.

2. Consider Your Audience: Understand your customer demographics, their preferences, and behaviors. Apply this knowledge to ascertain if a new trend aligns with your audience's needs, wants, and expectations.

3. Align with Business Goals: Every new trend you adopt should complement your overall business goals, brand image, and marketing strategy.

11.4. Leveraging Social Media Trends for Continued Success

When effectively leveraged, social media trends can provide remarkable results. They can help in reaching wider audiences, enhancing brand visibility, fostering customer relationships, and driving sales. However, it's essential to tactfully implement them to ensure they optimally serve your business goals. Here are some ideas:

1. Live Streaming and Virtual Reality: Live streaming creates opportunities for real-time interaction and provides an authentic experience for your audience. Similarly, virtual reality offers immersive experiences that can boost customer engagement and satisfaction.

2. User-Generated Content: Empowering customers to create content on behalf of your brand can strengthen their connection to your business, boost authenticity, and increase your reach.

3. Social Shopping: Social media platforms now offer in-app purchasing features. Utilizing these can streamline the buying process, resulting in an improved customer experience and increased conversion rates.

4. Collaborations with Influencers: Partnering with social media influencers who resonate with your brand can help you reach new audiences and strengthen your brand image.

5. Chatbots and Artificial Intelligence: Implementing AI-driven tools like Chatbots on your social media channels can enhance customer service, providing immediate responses and efficient resolution of customer queries.

11.5. Conclusion

Social media continues to be a powerful tool for retail businesses. However, the rapidly changing nature of these platforms necessitates vigilance and adaptability. Keeping pace with emerging trends allows companies to stay ahead of the curve and leverage new opportunities for growth and success. Understanding, evaluating, and incorporating these trends into your business model forms the basis for a future-proof social media strategy.

In business, as in life, change is the only constant. Embracing this reality and learning to navigate the ever-evolving social media landscape is an investment that will yield considerable dividends in the long run. Dive deep into the sea of social media, stay aware, stay informed, stay agile, and, most importantly, stay connected with your customers. They are, after all, the reason why you are in business.